Preface

Welcome to "The Physics of the Earth." This book is a journey through the fascinating world of Earth science, exploring the physical processes that shape our planet and influence life as we know it. From the depths of the oceans to the heights of the atmosphere, Earth is a dynamic and ever-changing environment, and understanding its physics is key to unlocking its mysteries.

In this book, we will delve into a wide range of topics, including Earth's structure and composition, plate tectonics, weather and climate, the water cycle, and the interactions between Earth and space. Each chapter offers a glimpse into the complexities of Earth's physics, providing insights into how our planet works and the forces that drive its behavior.

Whether you're a student, a science enthusiast, or simply curious about the world around you,

"The Physics of the Earth" offers something for everyone. Through clear explanations, engaging illustrations, and real-world examples, we aim to make complex scientific concepts accessible and understandable to readers of all backgrounds.

I hope that this book inspires you to explore further, to ask questions, and to deepen your understanding of the incredible planet we call home. Thank you for joining me on this journey through the physics of the Earth.

Charlie O. Williams
2024

TABLE OF CONTENT

THE PHYSICS OF THE EARTH:Unraveling the Mysteries of Our Dynamic Planet

Author
Charlie O. Williams

Introduction: Exploring the Wonders of Earth's Physics

Welcome, curious minds, to the fascinating world of Earth's physics! Have you ever looked up at the sky and wondered why the stars twinkle, or felt the ground shake beneath your feet during an earthquake? These are just a couple of the many mysteries that the physics of the Earth helps us understand.

In this book, we'll embark on an incredible journey to uncover the secrets of our planet—from the depths of its core to the vastness of its atmosphere. But before we dive into the exciting details, let's take a moment to think about what makes Earth so special.

Imagine Earth as a giant puzzle made up of countless pieces. Each piece—the land, the oceans, the air—is like a piece of the puzzle that fits together perfectly to create our home. But how did Earth become this way? And how does it all work together to sustain life?

To answer these questions, we need to understand the principles of Earth's physics. Physics is like the language of the universe—it helps us make sense of the world around us. Just as you learn to speak and understand your native language, we'll learn the language of Earth's physics to unlock its mysteries.

Our journey will take us deep underground, where we'll explore the layers of Earth's interior and discover what lies beneath our feet. We'll learn about the forces that shape our planet's surface, from the shifting of tectonic plates to the rumbling of volcanoes.

But our adventure doesn't stop there! We'll also soar high into the sky to study Earth's atmosphere and climate. We'll uncover the secrets of weather patterns, the science behind storms, and the delicate balance that keeps our planet's climate just right for life to thrive.

And as we journey through the pages of this book, we'll encounter other wonders of Earth's physics, from the swirling currents of the oceans to the shimmering lights of the auroras dancing in the night sky.

But why should we care about Earth's physics? Because understanding how our planet works is crucial for protecting it and ensuring a sustainable future for generations to come. By learning about Earth's physics, we can better understand the impacts of human activities on the environment and work together to find solutions.

So, are you ready to embark on this incredible journey? Grab your curiosity and join me as we dive into the captivating world of the physics of the Earth!

Chapter 1: Discovering Earth's Hidden Secrets

Imagine digging a hole in your backyard. As you dig deeper and deeper, you might find layers of soil, rocks, and maybe even some buried treasures like old toys or lost coins. But did you know that beneath the surface of the Earth, there's a whole world of wonders waiting to be discovered?

Digging Deep: Journey to Earth's Core

Let's start our adventure by digging deep underground to explore the hidden layers of Earth. The Earth's core is like the beating heart of our planet, pumping energy and heat to keep everything running smoothly. But what's it made of?

At the very center lies the inner core, a super-hot ball of solid iron and nickel. It's so hot down there that it would melt almost anything!

Surrounding the inner core is the outer core, a swirling sea of molten metal that generates Earth's magnetic field. This magnetic field acts like a giant shield, protecting us from harmful solar radiation.

As we move towards the surface, we encounter the mantle—a thick layer of hot, semi-solid rock. This is where all the action happens! The mantle is constantly churning and moving, like a pot of boiling soup. This movement is what drives tectonic plate motion and creates earthquakes and volcanoes.

Finally, we reach the Earth's crust—the thin outer layer that we call home. It's where mountains rise, valleys form, and oceans spread out as far as the eye can see. But did you know that the Earth's crust is actually made up of several large pieces called tectonic plates? These plates are always on the move, sliding past each other, colliding, or pulling apart.

Unraveling the Mysteries of Plate Tectonics

Now, let's zoom in on one of the most fascinating aspects of Earth's physics: plate tectonics. Imagine the Earth's crust as a giant jigsaw puzzle, with each piece constantly shifting and rearranging itself.

When two plates collide, they can create mighty mountain ranges like the Himalayas. When they pull apart, they form deep ocean trenches and volcanic islands. And when they slide past each other, they can trigger powerful earthquakes that shake the ground.

But why do these plates move? It's all because of the heat from the Earth's core. The hot mantle beneath the crust rises up towards the surface, causing the plates to drift apart. Then, as the mantle cools and sinks back down, it pulls the plates along with it.

Exploring Earth's Dynamic Surface

As we journey across the Earth's surface, we'll encounter a diverse range of landscapes—from towering mountains to vast plains, and from lush forests to barren deserts. Each of these landscapes tells a story of the powerful forces that have shaped our planet over millions of years.

But the Earth is not static—it's constantly changing and evolving. Volcanoes erupt, rivers carve deep valleys, and glaciers sculpt the land with their icy fingers. And through it all, the physics of the Earth is at work, shaping the world around us in ways both big and small.

So, as we continue our journey through the pages of this book, let's keep our eyes wide open and our minds ready to explore the hidden secrets of Earth's physics. Who knows what wonders we'll uncover next?

Chapter 2: The Mighty Forces of Earth's Magnetism

Have you ever played with a magnet and felt its invisible force pulling objects towards it? Well, did you know that our planet Earth has its own magnetic field, and it's even more powerful than any magnet you've ever seen?

The Mystery of Earth's Magnetic Field

Imagine Earth as a giant magnet, with invisible lines of force stretching out into space. This magnetic field surrounds our planet, protecting us from harmful solar radiation and guiding migratory animals like birds and turtles on their journeys.

But where does this magnetic field come from? The answer lies deep within the Earth's core. Remember how we talked about the swirling sea of molten metal in the outer core? Well, it turns out that this molten metal is constantly moving, like a giant conveyor belt. And as it moves, it generates electric currents that create Earth's magnetic field.

Navigating with Compasses and Magnetic Poles

One of the coolest things about Earth's magnetic field is that it helps us navigate our way around the world. Have you ever used a compass? It's a handy tool that always points towards the North Pole, thanks to the Earth's magnetic field.

But did you know that the magnetic poles aren't exactly the same as the geographic poles? That's right! The North Magnetic Pole and the South Magnetic Pole are actually located in slightly different places than the North and South Poles you see on maps.

Exploring the Auroras: Nature's Light Show

Now, let's journey to the far north or south, where something truly magical happens in the sky. Have you ever seen the northern lights, also known as the auroras? These dazzling displays of light dance across the sky in shades of green, purple, and red.

But what causes these breathtaking light shows? It all starts with the solar wind—a stream of charged particles that flows from the Sun towards the Earth. When these particles collide with the Earth's magnetic field, they create beautiful patterns of light in the sky.

Protecting Our Planet: The Importance of Earth's Magnetic Field

Earth's magnetic field is like a shield that protects us from the harmful effects of the solar wind and cosmic rays. Without it, life on Earth would be much more vulnerable to these powerful forces from space.

But our magnetic field is not invincible. It's constantly changing and shifting, and scientists are working hard to understand why. By studying Earth's magnetism, we can learn more about our planet's history and evolution, and perhaps even predict how the magnetic field might change in the future.

So, the next time you see a compass pointing north or catch a glimpse of the northern lights dancing in the sky, remember the mighty forces of Earth's magnetism at work all around us. And who knows? Maybe one day you'll join the ranks of scientists exploring the mysteries of our planet's magnetic field!

Chapter 3: Unveiling the Secrets of Earthquakes and Volcanoes

Have you ever felt the ground shake beneath your feet or seen a volcano erupting in the distance? These incredible events are part of the Earth's dynamic nature, driven by powerful forces deep within the planet.

The Trembling Earth: Exploring Earthquakes

Imagine standing on a giant puzzle, and suddenly, one of the pieces starts moving. That's what an earthquake feels like! Earthquakes are caused by the sudden release of energy along faults in the Earth's crust.

But what exactly is a fault? Think of it as a crack in the Earth's crust where two pieces of the puzzle meet. When stress builds up along these faults, it can cause them to suddenly slip and slide past each other, releasing energy in the form of seismic waves.

These seismic waves travel through the Earth, shaking the ground and causing buildings to sway and tremble. The strength of an earthquake is measured on a scale called the Richter scale, with stronger earthquakes causing more intense shaking and potential damage.

Fire from Below: The Power of Volcanoes

Now, let's turn our attention to another awe-inspiring natural phenomenon: volcanoes. Picture a mountain with a fiery heart, spewing out molten rock, ash, and gases into the sky. That's a volcano in action!

But how do volcanoes form? It all starts deep beneath the Earth's surface, where hot molten rock, called magma, collects in chambers below the crust. When the pressure builds up enough, the magma forces its way to the surface through cracks and vents, creating volcanic eruptions.

Volcanoes can be found all around the world, from towering peaks like Mount Vesuvius in Italy to underwater volcanoes hidden beneath the ocean's surface. Some eruptions are gentle, producing slow-moving lava flows, while others are explosive, sending ash and debris high into the sky.

Living with Earth's Fury

Living near earthquakes and volcanoes can be both thrilling and challenging. While these natural phenomena provide fertile soil for agriculture and geothermal energy, they also pose risks to communities and infrastructure.

But fear not! Scientists study earthquakes and volcanoes to better understand their behavior and develop ways to mitigate their impacts. Seismologists monitor ground movements to detect earthquakes before they strike, while volcanologists study volcanic activity to predict eruptions and evacuate at-risk areas.

By learning about earthquakes and volcanoes, we can prepare ourselves and our communities to respond effectively to these natural hazards. So, the next time the Earth rumbles or a volcano roars, remember the powerful forces at work beneath our feet, shaping the landscape and reminding us of the dynamic nature of our planet.

Chapter 4: Journey into the Heart of Earth's Mantle

Have you ever wondered what lies beneath the Earth's crust, beyond the fiery depths of volcanoes and the rumbling of earthquakes? Well, hold on tight as we embark on a journey deep into the heart of the Earth's mantle, where mysteries and wonders await!

The Mantle: Earth's Hidden Realm

Picture a thick, gooey layer of hot, semi-solid rock stretching for thousands of kilometers beneath your feet—that's the Earth's mantle! The mantle is like a giant conveyor belt, constantly moving and churning over millions of years.

But what makes the mantle move? It's all thanks to the heat from the Earth's core, which radiates outward and warms up the mantle from below. This creates a process called mantle convection,

where hot rock rises up towards the surface,
cools down, and then sinks back down again.

Unraveling the Mysteries of Mantle Convection

Imagine stirring a pot of soup on the stove. As you heat the soup from below, you'll notice that it starts to bubble and swirl. That's a bit like what happens in the Earth's mantle! The hot rock rises up towards the surface, creating upward currents, while the cooler rock sinks back down, creating downward currents.

This constant movement of rock within the mantle is what drives tectonic plate motion, volcanic activity, and even earthquakes. It's like a giant engine powering the dynamic processes that shape our planet's surface.

Peering Beneath the Surface: Seismic Waves and Earth's Interior

How do scientists study the Earth's mantle if it's hidden deep beneath the surface? Well, they use a clever tool called seismic waves. Just like how you can hear the rumble of thunder from a distant storm, seismic waves are vibrations that travel through the Earth and can be detected by sensitive instruments called seismometers.

By analyzing how seismic waves travel through the Earth, scientists can create images of the Earth's interior, much like taking an X-ray of your body at the doctor's office. These images help us understand the composition and structure of the mantle and uncover its hidden secrets.

Exploring the Great Unknown

Even though scientists have made incredible discoveries about the Earth's mantle, there's still so much we don't know. How hot is the mantle, and what is it made of? What role does the mantle play in shaping Earth's climate and environment over long periods of time?

These are just some of the questions that scientists are working hard to answer. By studying the Earth's mantle, we can unlock the secrets of our planet's past, present, and future—and perhaps even discover new wonders that we never knew existed.

So, as we journey deeper into the Earth's mantle, let's keep our minds open and our imaginations alive, ready to explore the mysteries of this hidden realm beneath our feet. Who knows what incredible discoveries await us in the heart of the Earth!

Chapter 5: Exploring Earth's Dynamic Atmosphere and Climate

Have you ever looked up at the sky and marveled at the ever-changing clouds, the warmth of the sun on your skin, or the gentle breeze blowing through the trees? Well, get ready to delve into the fascinating world of Earth's atmosphere and climate, where the air around us holds the secrets to our planet's weather and climate patterns!

The Breath of Life: Earth's Atmosphere

Imagine wrapping a cozy blanket around the Earth—that's a bit like what the atmosphere does! Earth's atmosphere is a thin layer of gases that surrounds our planet, providing us with the air we need to breathe and protecting us from the harshness of space.

But what exactly is the atmosphere made of? It's mostly nitrogen and oxygen, with a sprinkle of other gases like carbon dioxide, water vapor, and trace amounts of gases like argon and methane. These gases form a delicate balance that regulates Earth's temperature and weather patterns.

Weather Wonders: From Clouds to Storms

Have you ever watched clouds drifting across the sky and wondered how they form? Clouds are like floating cotton candy made of tiny water droplets or ice crystals suspended in the air. They form when warm, moist air rises into the atmosphere, cools down, and condenses into clouds.

But the atmosphere isn't always calm and peaceful—sometimes, it can be downright stormy! Thunderstorms, hurricanes, and tornadoes are just some of the wild weather phenomena that can occur when warm and cold air masses collide, creating powerful storms and swirling winds.

Climate: The Long-Term Picture

Now, let's zoom out and take a broader look at Earth's climate. Climate is like the average weather conditions in a particular region over a long period of time—think years, decades, or even centuries. It's influenced by factors like the sun's energy, the tilt of the Earth's axis, and the distribution of land and oceans.

But climate isn't the same everywhere on Earth. Different regions experience different climates, from the icy cold of the polar regions to the sweltering heat of the tropics. Climate scientists study these patterns to understand how our planet's climate is changing over time and what impact it might have on ecosystems and communities around the world.

Protecting Our Planet: The Role of Earth's Atmosphere and Climate

Earth's atmosphere and climate play a crucial role in supporting life on our planet. They regulate temperatures, provide us with clean air to breathe, and even help distribute nutrients and water around the globe.

But human activities, like burning fossil fuels and deforestation, are altering the composition of the atmosphere and disrupting Earth's climate patterns. By understanding how our actions affect the atmosphere and climate, we can work together to protect our planet and create a more sustainable future for all living beings.

So, the next time you step outside and feel the breeze on your face or watch a storm brewing on the horizon, take a moment to appreciate the wonders of Earth's atmosphere and climate—and remember that we all have a role to play in caring for our planet and preserving its beauty for future generations.

Chapter 6: Delving into the Mysteries of Earth's Oceans

Dive into the depths of Earth's oceans, where a world of wonders and mysteries awaits! From the shimmering surface to the dark abyss below, the oceans are teeming with life and hold secrets that scientists are still unraveling.

The Blue Planet: Exploring Earth's Oceans

Did you know that more than 70% of the Earth's surface is covered by oceans? That's right—our planet is truly a blue planet, with vast stretches of water stretching from pole to pole.

But what lies beneath the surface of the oceans? It's like exploring an alien world, filled with strange creatures, underwater mountains, and mysterious trenches that plunge to the deepest parts of the Earth.

Ocean Currents: The Heartbeat of the Sea

Imagine the oceans as giant conveyor belts, carrying warm water from the equator to the poles and cold water from the poles back to the equator. These ocean currents play a crucial role in regulating Earth's climate by distributing heat around the globe.

But what drives these ocean currents? It's a combination of factors, including the rotation of the Earth, differences in water temperature and salinity, and the shape of the ocean basins. Together, these forces create a complex network of currents that circulate water around the world.

Waves, Tides, and Currents: Forces of Nature

Have you ever stood on the beach and watched the waves crashing against the shore? Waves are like the heartbeat of the ocean, created by the wind blowing across the surface of the water. They can travel thousands of kilometers across the ocean before finally breaking on the shore.

Tides are another fascinating phenomenon caused by the gravitational pull of the Moon and the Sun. As the Earth rotates, the gravitational forces of the Moon and the Sun cause the water in the oceans to bulge outwards, creating high tides and low tides that rise and fall throughout the day.

Life in the Deep: Exploring the Ocean's Depths

Beneath the sunlit surface lies a world of darkness and mystery—the deep ocean. Here, strange and otherworldly creatures roam, from glowing jellyfish to giant squid with eyes the size of dinner plates.

But life in the deep ocean isn't easy. The pressure is intense, the temperatures are near freezing, and food can be scarce. Yet, somehow, life finds a way to thrive in this harsh environment, adapting to survive in ways that still baffle scientists.

Protecting Our Oceans: Guardians of the Deep

The oceans are not only home to a rich diversity of life but also play a vital role in regulating Earth's climate and providing resources for millions of people around the world. Yet, they are facing threats from pollution, overfishing, and climate change.

As stewards of our planet, it's up to us to protect our oceans and ensure their health and vitality for future generations. By reducing our carbon footprint, conserving marine habitats, and supporting sustainable fishing practices, we can all play a part in safeguarding the precious ecosystems of our oceans.

So, let's dive into the depths of Earth's oceans with wonder and curiosity, and remember to cherish and protect these magnificent and mysterious realms that sustain life on our blue planet.

Chapter 7: Exploring the Intricacies of Earth's Hydrology and Cryosphere

Let's embark on a journey to explore the watery realms of Earth's hydrology and the icy expanses of the cryosphere. From the rivers that flow through valleys to the glaciers that carve majestic mountains, these interconnected systems shape our planet's landscapes and play a vital role in supporting life.

The Hydrological Cycle: Earth's Water Dance

Imagine a never-ending dance of water, as it flows from the sky to the land, from rivers to oceans, and back again. This dance is known as the hydrological cycle, a continuous process that sustains life on Earth.

It begins with the Sun's energy heating the surface of the Earth, causing water to evaporate from oceans, lakes, and rivers into the atmosphere. This water vapor then condenses into clouds, which eventually release rain or snow back onto the land, replenishing rivers, lakes, and groundwater.

Rivers and Streams: Lifelines of the Land

Rivers and streams are like the arteries of the Earth, carrying life-giving water from the mountains to the sea. They carve deep valleys and canyons, provide habitats for countless species of plants and animals, and support human communities with water for drinking, irrigation, and transportation.

But rivers are more than just water—they also shape the land around them through erosion and deposition. Over time, rivers can carve out grand canyons and fertile floodplains, leaving behind a legacy of their meandering journey through the landscape.

Glaciers and Ice Sheets: Frozen Giants of the Earth

Now, let's turn our attention to the icy realms of the cryosphere, where glaciers and ice sheets reign supreme. These frozen giants store vast amounts of freshwater, shaping the landscape and influencing Earth's climate in profound ways.

Glaciers are like slow-moving rivers of ice, flowing downhill under their own weight. As they move, they carve deep valleys and fjords, leaving behind dramatic landscapes of towering peaks and sparkling ice. But glaciers are also sensitive indicators of climate change, shrinking in response to rising temperatures and altering river flows and water availability.

Groundwater: Earth's Hidden Reservoir

Beneath the surface lies another hidden treasure: groundwater. This is water that seeps down through the soil and rock, filling spaces and cracks underground. Groundwater is a vital source of freshwater for drinking, agriculture, and industry, providing a lifeline for communities in arid regions and during droughts.

But groundwater is not an infinite resource—it can be depleted through overuse or contaminated by pollution from human activities. That's why it's important to manage groundwater wisely and protect it from contamination to ensure its availability for future generations.

Caring for Earth's Water Resources

As stewards of our planet, it's up to us to protect and conserve Earth's water resources for the benefit of all living beings. By practicing water conservation, reducing pollution, and promoting sustainable water management practices, we can ensure that future generations inherit a healthy and vibrant planet.

So, let's marvel at the wonders of Earth's hydrology and cryosphere, and pledge to cherish and protect these precious resources that sustain life on our blue planet.

Chapter 8: Unveiling the Secrets of Environmental Geophysics

Welcome to the fascinating world of environmental geophysics, where science meets exploration to uncover the hidden secrets of our planet's surface and subsurface. From hunting for hidden treasures underground to monitoring environmental changes from above, environmental geophysics offers a window into Earth's mysteries.

The Science of Seeing Underground

Imagine having X-ray vision that allows you to see beneath the Earth's surface—that's a bit like what environmental geophysics does! Using a variety of tools and techniques, scientists can peer into the ground to map out what lies beneath, from buried archaeological sites to underground water reservoirs.

One of the most common methods used in environmental geophysics is called ground-penetrating radar (GPR). This technique sends out pulses of electromagnetic waves into the ground and measures the reflections that bounce back, revealing hidden objects and structures underground.

Unearthing Hidden Treasures

Have you ever dreamed of discovering buried treasure like a pirate from a storybook? Well, environmental geophysicists do just that—except instead of gold and jewels, they're searching for things like ancient artifacts, buried pipelines, and even lost shipwrecks!

By analyzing the data collected from techniques like GPR and magnetometry, scientists can create detailed maps of the subsurface and pinpoint the locations of buried objects with remarkable accuracy. It's like solving a giant puzzle where the pieces are hidden underground!

Monitoring Earth's Vital Signs

But environmental geophysics isn't just about digging holes and searching for buried treasures—it's also about keeping an eye on the health of our planet. Scientists use geophysical techniques to monitor environmental changes, like land subsidence, groundwater depletion, and soil contamination.

For example, satellites equipped with sensors can measure changes in the Earth's surface over time, such as the sinking of land due to groundwater extraction or the expansion of urban areas. This information helps scientists track environmental trends and develop strategies for sustainable land management.

Protecting Our Planet for Future Generations

As stewards of our planet, it's up to us to protect and preserve Earth's resources for future generations. By harnessing the power of environmental geophysics, we can better understand the challenges facing our planet and develop innovative solutions to address them.

Whether it's mapping out underground resources, monitoring environmental changes, or protecting cultural heritage sites, environmental geophysics plays a crucial role in safeguarding Earth's treasures. So, let's continue to explore, discover, and protect the wonders of our planet, together!

Bridging Science and Society

Environmental geophysics isn't just confined to the realm of scientists and researchers—it also has important applications in society. For example, environmental geophysics is used in construction projects to assess the stability of building sites and detect potential hazards like sinkholes or underground utilities.

Similarly, it plays a key role in natural resource exploration, helping companies locate mineral deposits, oil and gas reserves, and groundwater sources in an environmentally responsible manner. By using geophysical methods, companies can minimize their environmental impact and ensure sustainable resource extraction.

Exploring New Frontiers

As technology advances and our understanding of Earth's processes deepens, the field of environmental geophysics continues to evolve and expand. Scientists are constantly developing new techniques and tools to explore previously inaccessible regions, from the depths of the ocean to the icy expanses of Antarctica.

One exciting area of research is using geophysical methods to study the impacts of climate change on Earth's polar regions. By monitoring changes in ice thickness, temperature, and sea level, scientists can better understand the dynamics of ice sheets and predict how they will respond to a warming climate.

Inspiring the Next Generation

Perhaps most importantly, environmental geophysics inspires curiosity and wonder about the world around us. By engaging students and the public in hands-on activities and field trips, scientists and educators can spark a lifelong interest in Earth science and environmental stewardship.

After all, the future of our planet depends on the next generation of scientists, engineers, and decision-makers who will tackle the environmental challenges of tomorrow. By instilling a sense of wonder and appreciation for Earth's treasures, environmental geophysics can empower young minds to become the guardians of our planet's future.

Conclusion

In conclusion, environmental geophysics offers a fascinating glimpse into the hidden secrets of our planet's surface and subsurface. From uncovering buried treasures to monitoring environmental changes, this interdisciplinary field bridges the gap between science and society, inspiring curiosity and fostering stewardship of our planet's resources.

As we continue to explore and discover the wonders of Earth's environment, let us remember the importance of protecting and preserving these treasures for future generations. By working together, we can ensure that our planet remains a vibrant and thriving home for all living beings.

Chapter 9: Earth and Space Interaction: Exploring the Cosmic Connection

Get ready to blast off into space as we embark on a thrilling journey to explore the fascinating interactions between Earth and the cosmos beyond. From the dazzling lights of the auroras to the impact of space weather on our planet, the relationship between Earth and space is full of wonders waiting to be discovered.

The Dance of Earth and Sun

Imagine the Earth and the Sun as dance partners in a never-ending cosmic ballet. The Sun shines brightly, sending out streams of light and energy that warm our planet and nourish life. But did you know that the Sun also affects Earth in other ways?

One of the most noticeable effects is the changing seasons. As the Earth orbits around the

Sun, its axis is tilted relative to its orbit, causing different parts of the Earth to receive varying amounts of sunlight throughout the year. This tilt creates the seasons we experience, from the warmth of summer to the chill of winter.

Lights in the Sky: Exploring the Auroras

Have you ever gazed up at the night sky and seen shimmering curtains of light dancing across the darkness? These magical displays are known as the auroras, and they occur when charged particles from the Sun collide with Earth's atmosphere.

The most famous auroras are the northern lights, or aurora borealis, which can be seen in the polar regions of the Northern Hemisphere. But did you know that there are also southern lights, or aurora australis, in the Southern Hemisphere? These breathtaking light shows are a reminder of the interconnectedness of Earth and space.

Space Weather: The Sun's Influence on Earth

While the Sun provides us with warmth and light, it can also unleash powerful storms and eruptions of solar material into space. These events, known as space weather, can have a dramatic impact on Earth's atmosphere and technology.

For example, solar flares and coronal mass ejections can send bursts of radiation and charged particles towards Earth, causing disruptions to satellite communications, power grids, and even airline routes. Understanding and monitoring space weather is crucial for protecting our technology and infrastructure from these solar storms.

Earth's Magnetosphere: Our Cosmic Shield

But fear not! Earth is protected by a mighty shield known as the magnetosphere, which deflects and traps harmful solar radiation and charged particles from the Sun. This invisible force field extends far out into space, creating a protective bubble around our planet.

The magnetosphere is like a giant magnetic bubble that surrounds Earth, created by the interaction between the Earth's magnetic field and the solar wind. It acts like a shield, deflecting most of the solar particles away from our planet and protecting us from the harmful effects of space weather.

Exploring Beyond Earth: The Future of Space Exploration

As we continue to explore the wonders of space and unlock the mysteries of the cosmos, it's important to remember our connection to Earth and the impact that space has on our planet. Whether it's studying the auroras from space or monitoring space weather from the ground, scientists are constantly learning more about the dynamic relationship between Earth and space.

And who knows what the future holds? Perhaps one day, humans will venture beyond Earth to explore other planets and moons in our solar system and beyond. But no matter how far we travel, Earth will always be our home, a precious oasis in the vastness of space.

Protecting Earth's Fragile Balance

As we marvel at the wonders of space and our cosmic connection, it's essential to remember the delicate balance that exists between Earth and the universe. While space offers us countless opportunities for exploration and discovery, it also presents challenges and threats to our planet's well-being.

For example, the increasing amount of space debris orbiting Earth poses a risk to satellites and spacecraft, and the potential for collisions could create even more debris, leading to a dangerous cascade effect known as the Kessler syndrome. Additionally, the growing interest in space mining and commercial space travel raises questions about the long-term sustainability and environmental impact of human activities in space.

Harnessing Space for the Benefit of Earth

Despite these challenges, space also offers opportunities to address pressing global issues and improve life on Earth. Satellites provide essential data for weather forecasting, climate monitoring, disaster response, and navigation, helping us better understand and manage Earth's resources and environment.

Furthermore, space exploration inspires innovation and collaboration, driving advances in technology, science, and engineering that benefit society as a whole. From medical breakthroughs to sustainable energy solutions, the knowledge and technologies developed through space exploration have the potential to transform our world for the better.

Looking to the Stars: Our Cosmic Destiny

As we gaze up at the night sky and ponder the mysteries of the universe, let us remember our place in the cosmos and our responsibility to cherish and protect our home planet. Earth is not just a speck of dust in the vastness of space—it's a precious oasis of life, a beacon of hope in the darkness.

By nurturing a sense of wonder and curiosity about the cosmos, we can inspire future generations to explore, discover, and protect the wonders of our planet and beyond. Together, let us continue to reach for the stars while standing firmly grounded on the solid foundation of Earth, our one and only home.

Chapter 10: The Future of Earth's Physics: Innovations and Challenges Ahead

As we come to the final chapter of our journey through the physics of the Earth, let's peer into the crystal ball and glimpse the future of our planet's scientific exploration. From cutting-edge innovations to pressing challenges, the road ahead is filled with excitement and uncertainty.

Innovations on the Horizon

Imagine a world where robots roam the ocean depths, drones soar through the skies, and satellites orbit the Earth, collecting data and unlocking the secrets of our planet's physics. This future is closer than you might think, thanks to advances in technology and scientific research.

For example, autonomous underwater vehicles (AUVs) equipped with sensors and cameras can explore the ocean's depths with unprecedented precision, mapping out underwater landscapes and studying marine life. Similarly, drones and satellites provide valuable insights into Earth's atmosphere, climate, and environmental changes from above.

Artificial Intelligence: The Power of Data

But it's not just about collecting data—it's about what we do with it. That's where artificial intelligence (AI) comes in. By harnessing the power of AI and machine learning, scientists can analyze vast amounts of data more quickly and accurately than ever before, uncovering patterns and insights that were once hidden.

For example, AI algorithms can predict natural disasters like earthquakes and hurricanes with greater accuracy, giving communities more time to prepare and evacuate. They can also optimize energy usage, improve agricultural productivity, and even help diagnose and treat diseases.

Climate Change: The Urgency of Action

However, the future of Earth's physics is not without its challenges. Perhaps the most pressing of these challenges is climate change, driven by human activities like burning fossil fuels, deforestation, and industrial pollution.

Climate change poses a threat to ecosystems, biodiversity, and human societies around the world, with consequences ranging from rising sea levels and extreme weather events to food and water shortages. Addressing this global challenge requires collective action and commitment from governments, businesses, and individuals alike.

Sustainable Solutions for a Brighter Future

But there is hope on the horizon. From renewable energy sources like solar and wind power to sustainable agriculture practices and conservation efforts, there are countless ways we can mitigate the impacts of climate change and build a more sustainable future for our planet.

By investing in clean energy technologies, protecting natural habitats, and reducing our carbon footprint, we can create a world where future generations can thrive in harmony with nature. It's a daunting task, but it's also an opportunity to come together as a global community and chart a course towards a brighter tomorrow.

Conclusion: Our Shared Responsibility

As we look ahead to the future of Earth's physics, let us remember that we all have a role to play in shaping the destiny of our planet. Whether it's through scientific research, technological innovation, or everyday actions like recycling and conserving energy, each of us has the power to make a difference.

So, let's embrace the challenges and opportunities that lie ahead with optimism and determination. Together, we can unlock the mysteries of the universe, protect the wonders of our planet, and ensure a prosperous future for generations to come. After all, Earth is not just our home—it's our shared legacy, our common bond, and our greatest treasure.

Embracing Diversity and Collaboration

As we navigate the complexities of Earth's physics and chart a course for the future, let us also embrace diversity and collaboration as guiding principles. Science knows no borders, and the challenges we face—from climate change to environmental degradation—require global solutions that transcend political and cultural divides.

By fostering collaboration among scientists, policymakers, educators, and communities around the world, we can harness the collective wisdom and expertise of diverse perspectives to tackle the most pressing issues of our time. Together, we can build a more inclusive and sustainable world where every voice is heard, and every contribution is valued.

Inspiring the Next Generation of Explorers

As we pass the torch to the next generation of scientists, explorers, and stewards of our planet, let us inspire them with the wonders of Earth's physics and the boundless possibilities of scientific discovery. By nurturing their curiosity, creativity, and passion for learning, we can empower them to shape a brighter future for humanity and the natural world.

Through hands-on experiences, mentorship programs, and STEM education initiatives, we can ignite the spark of curiosity and instill a sense of wonder in young minds, encouraging them to dream big and reach for the stars. After all, the future belongs to those who dare to imagine, explore, and innovate.

A Call to Action

In closing, let us heed the call to action and rise to the challenges and opportunities that lie ahead. Whether it's through scientific research, technological innovation, environmental advocacy, or grassroots activism, each of us has a role to play in shaping the future of Earth's physics and safeguarding the planet for future generations.

Let us come together as stewards of our planet, united by a shared vision of a sustainable and thriving world where humanity lives in harmony with nature. By working together with courage, compassion, and determination, we can overcome any obstacle and build a future worthy of our children and grandchildren.

So, let us embark on this journey with hope in our hearts, curiosity in our minds, and a commitment to leaving a positive legacy for generations to come. Together, we can unlock the mysteries of the universe, protect the wonders of our planet, and ensure a bright and prosperous future for all.

Chapter 11: Earth's Endless Wonder: Exploring the Frontiers of Discovery

Welcome to the final chapter of our adventure through the physics of the Earth! As we conclude our journey, let's reflect on the endless wonder and boundless potential that our planet holds. From the depths of the oceans to the heights of the atmosphere, Earth continues to surprise and inspire us with its beauty and complexity.

The Quest for Knowledge

Imagine Earth as a giant puzzle, with each piece representing a different aspect of its physics—its atmosphere, oceans, landforms, and more. Scientists are like detectives, piecing together clues and unraveling mysteries to understand how our planet works and how it's changing over time.

But the quest for knowledge is never-ending. There are still so many unanswered questions waiting to be explored. What lies at the bottom of the deepest ocean trench? How do clouds form and rain fall from the sky? What secrets are hidden in the far reaches of the universe beyond our planet?

Embracing Wonder and Curiosity

One of the most beautiful things about science is its ability to spark wonder and curiosity in our hearts and minds. Whether it's watching a sunset paint the sky with a palette of colors or marveling at the intricate patterns of a snowflake, there's magic to be found in every corner of our planet.

By embracing wonder and curiosity, we open ourselves up to new possibilities and discoveries. We become explorers of our own world, eager to learn and grow with each new experience. So, let's never lose our sense of wonder, for it is the fuel that drives us forward on our journey of discovery.

Protecting Earth's Treasures

As we explore the frontiers of discovery, it's important to remember our responsibility to protect and preserve Earth's treasures for future generations. From the towering redwoods of California to the coral reefs of the Great Barrier Reef, our planet is home to a rich diversity of life and landscapes that must be cherished and safeguarded.

That's why conservation efforts are so vital. By protecting natural habitats, reducing pollution, and combating climate change, we can ensure that Earth's wonders continue to inspire and delight us for generations to come. After all, we only have one planet—it's up to us to take care of it.

The Power of One

You might be wondering, "What can I do to make a difference?" The truth is, even the smallest actions can have a big impact. Whether it's picking up litter at the beach, planting a tree in your backyard, or simply taking the time to appreciate the beauty of nature, every little bit helps.

By working together and taking action, we can create positive change in the world. So, let's stand up for our planet and be champions of Earth's endless wonder. Together, we can make a difference and leave a legacy of stewardship and sustainability for future generations to inherit.

Conclusion: A Journey of Discovery

As we bid farewell to our journey through the physics of the Earth, let's remember the lessons we've learned and the wonders we've encountered along the way. From the depths of the ocean to the vastness of space, Earth is a treasure trove of discovery, waiting to be explored and celebrated.

So, let's continue to marvel at the beauty of our planet, to question and to wonder, and to strive for a future where Earth's endless wonder is preserved and protected for all. Thank you for joining me on this incredible adventure. Until we meet again, keep exploring, keep dreaming, and keep embracing the wonder of our amazing planet.

Chapter 12: Earth-Space Interaction: Exploring the Dynamic Relationship

Welcome to the final chapter of our exploration into the physics of the Earth. In this chapter, we'll delve deep into the dynamic relationship between Earth and space, uncovering the intricate connections and fascinating phenomena that shape our planet's interaction with the cosmos beyond.

The Dance of Earth and Space

Imagine Earth as a dancer twirling gracefully through the cosmic ballet of space. As our planet orbits the Sun, it interacts with a myriad of cosmic forces, from the gentle tug of the Moon's gravity to the powerful storms of solar activity emanating from our closest star.

But the dance doesn't end there. Earth's atmosphere extends far out into space, mingling with the solar wind and cosmic rays that permeate the universe. This interaction creates a dynamic and ever-changing environment where Earth and space are inextricably linked.

Solar Influence: The Power of the Sun

At the heart of Earth-space interaction lies the Sun, our primary source of light, heat, and energy. The Sun's radiant energy drives the processes that sustain life on our planet, from photosynthesis in plants to the water cycle that replenishes our rivers and oceans.

But the Sun is also a powerful force that can influence Earth's environment in dramatic ways. Solar flares, coronal mass ejections, and other solar phenomena can send bursts of radiation and charged particles hurtling towards our planet, disrupting communications, damaging satellites, and even creating dazzling displays of auroras in the polar regions.

Earth's Magnetic Shield: Protecting Against Space Weather

Fortunately, Earth is equipped with a powerful defense mechanism against the onslaught of solar activity: the magnetosphere. This invisible shield, generated by the Earth's magnetic field, deflects and traps charged particles from the Sun, preventing them from reaching the surface of our planet.

The magnetosphere acts like a protective bubble around Earth, shielding us from the harmful effects of space weather while allowing essential particles like solar wind to interact with our atmosphere and create phenomena like auroras. Without this shield, life on Earth would be far more vulnerable to the ravages of cosmic radiation.

Exploring the Unknown: Earth's Cosmic Neighborhood

Beyond the protective embrace of the magnetosphere lies the vast expanse of space, waiting to be explored and understood. From the mysteries of the lunar surface to the distant planets of our solar system and beyond, there are endless opportunities for discovery and adventure in Earth's cosmic neighborhood.

Robotic spacecraft and satellites have ventured far from Earth, sending back stunning images and valuable data that shed light on the secrets of the universe. Whether it's studying the geology of Mars, probing the icy moons of Jupiter, or searching for signs of life on distant exoplanets, humanity's exploration of space is driven by an insatiable curiosity to understand our place in the cosmos.

The Future of Earth-Space Exploration

As we look to the future, the relationship between Earth and space will continue to evolve and inspire new generations of scientists, engineers, and explorers. From establishing sustainable colonies on other planets to harnessing the abundant resources of the solar system, humanity's dreams of space exploration are limited only by our imagination and ingenuity.

But with great opportunity comes great responsibility. As we venture further into space, we must ensure that our exploration is conducted with respect for the environments we encounter and with a commitment to preserving the delicate balance of Earth's ecosystems.

Conclusion: A Cosmic Connection

In conclusion, the relationship between Earth and space is a complex and dynamic interplay of forces that shapes the environment of our planet and inspires wonder and exploration. From the life-giving energy of the Sun to the protective embrace of the magnetosphere, Earth's cosmic connection is a testament to the beauty and complexity of the universe.

As we continue to explore and understand the mysteries of Earth and space, let us remember that we are all interconnected inhabitants of a vast and wondrous cosmos. By embracing curiosity, collaboration, and stewardship, we can unlock the secrets of the universe and ensure a bright and prosperous future for generations to come. Thank you for joining me on this incredible journey through the physics of the Earth. Until we meet again, may the wonders of the cosmos continue to inspire and awe us all.

Chapter 13: The Fragile Balance of Earth's Climate

Welcome to the final chapter of our exploration into the physics of the Earth. In this chapter, we'll delve into the delicate balance of Earth's climate, uncovering the factors that influence it and the challenges we face in preserving it for future generations.

Understanding Earth's Climate

Imagine Earth's climate as a giant puzzle, with pieces scattered across the globe. Each piece represents a different aspect of our planet's climate—temperature, precipitation, wind patterns, and more. Together, these pieces form a complex and interconnected system that regulates the conditions on our planet.

But understanding Earth's climate is no easy task. It's like trying to solve a puzzle with missing pieces and pieces that keep changing shape. Scientists study past climate records, collect data from satellites and weather stations, and use computer models to simulate Earth's climate and predict future changes.

The Greenhouse Effect: Earth's Blanket

One of the key factors that regulates Earth's climate is the greenhouse effect. Imagine Earth's atmosphere as a cozy blanket wrapped around the planet, trapping heat from the Sun and keeping our planet warm. This blanket is made up of gases like carbon dioxide, methane, and water vapor, which absorb and re-radiate heat energy.

But like any blanket, too much of it can make us uncomfortably warm. Human activities like burning fossil fuels, deforestation, and industrial processes have increased the concentration of greenhouse gases in the atmosphere, thickening Earth's blanket and trapping more heat. This leads to global warming and climate change, with consequences like rising temperatures, melting ice caps, and extreme weather events.

The Role of Feedback Loops

To make things even more complicated, Earth's climate is influenced by feedback loops—interactions between different parts of the climate system that can amplify or dampen the effects of climate change. For example, melting ice exposes darker surfaces like water or land, which absorb more sunlight and cause further warming—a positive feedback loop.

On the other hand, increased cloud cover can reflect more sunlight back into space, cooling the planet—a negative feedback loop. Understanding these feedback mechanisms is essential for predicting how Earth's climate will respond to human activities and natural processes in the future.

The Impacts of Climate Change

Climate change is already having a profound impact on our planet and the people and animals that call it home. From rising sea levels threatening coastal communities to more frequent and intense heatwaves, storms, and wildfires, the effects of climate change are being felt around the world.

But it's not just about the environment—climate change also affects our health, our food and water supply, our economies, and our way of life. Vulnerable communities, including low-income populations, indigenous peoples, and small island nations, are often hit the hardest by the impacts of climate change, exacerbating existing inequalities and injustices.

Taking Action for a Sustainable Future

The good news is that we still have time to address climate change and mitigate its worst effects. By reducing our greenhouse gas emissions, transitioning to renewable energy sources, conserving natural habitats, and adapting to the changes that are already happening, we can build a more sustainable and resilient future for ourselves and future generations.

But we can't do it alone. Addressing climate change requires collective action and cooperation at all levels of society—from individuals and communities to governments and international organizations. By working together, we can create a world where everyone has access to clean air, clean water, and a healthy environment.

Conclusion: A Call to Action

In conclusion, the fragile balance of Earth's climate is one of the greatest challenges facing humanity today. But it's also an opportunity for us to come together, to innovate, and to create a better world for ourselves and future generations.

As stewards of our planet, it's up to us to take action to protect and preserve Earth's climate for the sake of all life on Earth. Whether it's reducing our carbon footprint, advocating for climate policies, or supporting sustainable practices in our communities, each of us has a role to play in shaping the future of our planet.

So let's rise to the challenge, let's embrace the opportunity, and let's work together to build a brighter, more sustainable future for all. Thank you for joining me on this journey through the physics of the Earth. Together, we can make a difference.

Chapter 14: Exploring Earth's Dynamic Landscapes

Welcome to the final chapter of our journey through the physics of the Earth. In this chapter, we'll dive into the diverse and dynamic landscapes that make up our planet's surface, from towering mountains to vast oceans, and everything in between.

The Earth's Canvas: Landforms and Features

Imagine Earth as a giant canvas, painted with a kaleidoscope of colors, shapes, and textures. Each brushstroke represents a different landform or feature, shaped by the forces of nature over millions of years. From the rugged peaks of the

Himalayas to the rolling plains of the Midwest, Earth's landscapes are a testament to the beauty and power of geological processes.

But how did these landscapes form? It's a bit like a sculptor carving a masterpiece out of stone. Earth's landforms are shaped by a variety of processes, including erosion by wind and water, volcanic activity, tectonic movements, and the slow but steady march of time. Over millennia, these forces have sculpted and molded the Earth's surface into the breathtaking landscapes we see today.

The Power of Water: Shaping Earth's Surface

Water is one of the most powerful agents of change on Earth's surface. From gentle streams to raging rivers, from tranquil lakes to mighty oceans, water shapes the land in countless ways. Erosion by water can carve deep valleys, create dramatic cliffs and canyons, and even form massive cave systems hidden beneath the Earth's surface.

But water doesn't just shape the land—it also sustains life. Rivers provide water for drinking, irrigation, and transportation, while oceans support a vast array of ecosystems and play a crucial role in regulating Earth's climate. Without water, life as we know it would not exist.

The Drama of Tectonic Activity

Beneath the surface of the Earth, another powerful force is at work: tectonic activity. The Earth's crust is divided into a series of large plates that float on the semi-fluid mantle beneath them. These plates are constantly moving, colliding, and sliding past each other, creating earthquakes, volcanic eruptions, and mountain ranges in the process.

Tectonic activity is responsible for shaping many of the Earth's most iconic landscapes, from the towering peaks of the Andes to the deep trenches of the ocean floor. It's a reminder of the dynamic and ever-changing nature of our planet, where geological forces continue to shape and reshape the landscape over time.

The Impact of Human Activity

But human activity is also leaving its mark on Earth's landscapes. Deforestation, urbanization, mining, and agriculture are altering the natural environment at an unprecedented rate, leading to habitat loss, soil erosion, and pollution. These changes threaten not only the beauty and diversity of Earth's landscapes but also the health and well-being of ecosystems and communities around the world.

As stewards of our planet, it's up to us to protect and preserve Earth's landscapes for future generations. By adopting sustainable practices, conserving natural habitats, and embracing the principles of environmental stewardship, we can ensure that Earth's landscapes remain a source of inspiration and wonder for centuries to come.

Conclusion: A Living Tapestry

In conclusion, Earth's landscapes are a living tapestry, woven together by the forces of nature and the hand of humanity. From the majestic mountains to the tranquil valleys, from the rolling plains to the endless seas, each landscape tells a story of resilience, adaptation, and interconnectedness.

As we marvel at the beauty and diversity of Earth's landscapes, let us remember our responsibility to protect and preserve them for future generations. By working together, we can ensure that Earth's landscapes remain a source of inspiration and wonder for all who call our planet home.

Thank you for joining me on this journey through the physics of the Earth. May the beauty and majesty of Earth's landscapes continue to inspire and awe us all.

Acknowledgements

This book would not have been possible without the support, guidance, and contributions of many individuals and organizations.

First and foremost, I would like to express my heartfelt gratitude to all the scientists, researchers, and educators whose tireless work and dedication have deepened our understanding of the physics of the Earth. Your passion for discovery and commitment to excellence have inspired me throughout this journey.

I am also grateful to my family and friends for their unwavering encouragement and support.

Your love and belief in me have sustained me through the challenges and joys of writing this book.

I extend my appreciation to the publishers, editors, and production team who helped bring this book to life. Your professionalism and expertise have been invaluable in shaping the final product.

Additionally, I would like to thank the readers and enthusiasts who share my passion for Earth science. Your curiosity and enthusiasm drive me to continue exploring and sharing the wonders of our planet.

Lastly, I dedicate this book to the Earth itself, our precious home and the source of endless inspiration. May we cherish and protect it for generations to come.

Thank you all for being a part of this incredible journey.

Warm regards,

Charlie O. Williams